DOG LOVE

BY **K. R. WARD**

ILLUSTRATED BY **MARIŽAN**

BIBLIOKID
PUBLISHING

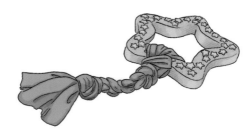

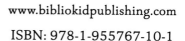

To my Aunt Ashley,
who never gave up on me. –KW

For Isabella, the person with
the biggest heart. –MR

Look at your dog sitting there.
He's such a good boy!

You know he loves you because of . . .

those big puppy-dog eyes,

a swishing tail,

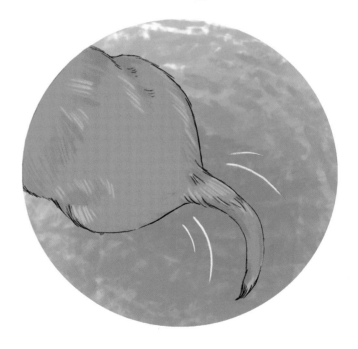

and . . .

WET KISSES!

Your dog loves you more than anything.
But how can you show him you love him just as much?

By doing his favorite activities together!

Race through the park.

Play fetch.

Try tug-of-war with a stick.

Just don't forget the . . .

TREATS!

Treats are good to teach him amazing tricks.

Or for hide and seek.

And to keep him healthy.

Give your dog good food and clean water every day.

Never give him people food.

Especially chocolate!

Brush his fur so his coat shines.

Give your dog a bath. But be prepared . . .

You might get wet!

The easiest way to show your dog you love him
is with snuggles and affection!

No matter how big

or small they are . . .

Every dog wants to be
LOVED!

If you follow these steps, your dog will always know you love him.

FUN FACTS ABOUT DOGS

The most popular dog breed in the United States is the Labrador Retriever.

Labrador Retriever

The smallest dog breed is the Chihuahua.

Chihuahua

English Mastiff

The largest dog breed is the English Mastiff.

The dog breed with the softest fur is the Chow Chow.

Chow Chow

Border Collie

Greyhound

The Border Collie is
the smartest dog breed.

The dog breed that can run
the fastest is the Greyhound.

German Shepherd

The dog breed with the
strongest sense of smell
is the Bloodhound.

One of the strongest dog breeds
is the German Shepherd.

Bloodhound

ABOUT THE AUTHOR

KATELYN WARD found inspiration for *Dog Love* in her ardent love for animals, especially dogs. She wrote this book, not only to foster empathy in young readers, but also to expand their knowledge of different dog breeds. Sometimes the fastest way to heal a heart is by loving a four-legged friend and by letting them love you. This book is for young readers to begin to understand the relationship between love and responsibility.

ABOUT THE ILLUSTRATOR

MARIŽAN (Maja Ranisavljev) is an illustrator who enjoys creating for those who cherish the imaginative playful spirit. Maja loves to move people with colors and astonish them by involving compositions; she finds inspiration for her illustrations in every corner of the world. She lives in Pančevo, a town in Serbia, with her family in a home full of books, plants, and toys.